In My Time

James T. Slattery

First printed by CreateSpace 10/01/16

ISBN-13: 978-1537420509
ISBN-10: 153742050X

Cover Art: Paul Gavarni, Le Flâneur, 1842.

Printed in the United States of America

Also by James T. Slattery

Camp Life in the Northern Kingdom Series:

Memories of Frosty Mornings and Cold Nights in the Company of Men

and

An Adirondack Sanctuary

The Warrior Life

The Warrior Life Field Manual

The Adam Commission

Menaissance Journal

Dedication

This book is dedicated to the memory of a Warrior.

PFC DONALD J. SLATTERY, 32377286
Third Infantry Division
15th Infantry Regiment
F Company Medical Detachment
KIA: 1 March 1944, Anzio Beachhead

Donald J. Slattery is on the far right.

Contents

Preface

"All the world's a stage, and all the men and women merely players..."
As You Like It, Shakespeare

This book contains scenes from an opera called "My Life" featuring actors who didn't know they were acting while reciting a script they didn't existed.

These scenes were acted-out over a ten-year period in public places where a goodly amount of life is lived.

My role in this opera was a Flâneur or "Stroller", "Lounger", "Saunterer", or "Loafer".

I observed the scenes without the actors' knowledge. In modern parlance I was a "Third-party Observer" functioning at the "Meta-level".

> **Opera** is an art form in which singers and musicians perform a dramatic work combining text (libretto) and musical score, usually in a theatrical setting.
> Wikipedia

> **Flâneur** from the French noun flâneur, means "stroller", "lounger", "saunterer", or "loafer". Flânerie refers to the act of strolling, with all of its accompanying associations.
> Wikipedia

I hope you enjoy the scenes and that you learn something about the human condition and most importantly I hope you see the Humor in "My Life".

Your most humble servant,

jim

Notes:

The title of this work – "In My Time" – is homage to Ernest Hemingway's classic work, "In Our Time", which is his first collection of short stories published in 1925 by Boni & Liveright, New York.

https://en.wikipedia.org/wiki/In_Our_Time_(short_story_colle ction)

For a more detailed explanation of a Flâneur go to:
https://en.wikipedia.org/wiki/Fl%C3%A2neur

Don't Have a "Passion" to Make a Difference

I'm begging you don't have a "passion" to make a difference.

First of all the only passion I have is for women. I don't have a passion to be a wage slave for a corporation, to sell or provide insurance, fix your car, sell you stuff, listen to your crap and act like I care, to clean your carpets or home, to provide you with personal services of any kind, etc. and in the same vein the only family I have is the one I was born or married into.

I don't want to join your family of companies, to hold one of your family of debit or credit cards, eat at your restaurant making me a member of your restaurant family, and/or buy gas or other products or services which compels me to be a member of your shallow and exploitive marketing concept of a family.

Secondly, I just want to be left alone. Graduation speeches and commercials feature young people who say they have a passion to make a difference. Well let me share something with you. I don't want to be involved with your "passion" to make a difference because in my experience the new boss is the same as the old boss and what you think is a positive change has unintended consequences which you have a limited capacity to predict, understand, or remediate and if even if you could you'd still go ahead and do whatever you're contemplating.

In My Time

And finally, in case I've not adequately communicated what I think I'll make it simple so that even a Liberal can understand. I want to be left alone. I don't want you to change something because you've been programmed to do so. I don't know how many times I've heard of some new program or other that's supposed to fix some problem that I didn't know exists yet I'm told it's a serious situation and I should be thankful that some politician or youngster is dedicating their lives to the passionate resolution of said problem.

Here's a new concept; how about we have legions of people who have a "passion" to leave me alone and maintain the status quo. How's that? Educate people to manage things that maintain our infrastructure, social programs, or economic activities, and just leave me the hell alone.

Say You're Welcome

The following are Traditional and Modern social transactions.

Traditional
Actor 1: "Can I help you?"
Actor 2: "Yes two tacos please."
Actor 1   Gets tacos.
Actor 1: "Anything else?"
Actor 2: "No thank you."
Actor 1: **"You're welcome."**

Modern
Actor 1: "Can I help you?"
Actor 2: "Yes two tacos please."
Actor 1   Gets tacos.
Actor 1: "Anything else?"
Actor 2: "No thank you."
Actor 1: **"No problem."**

What's the Difference?
The **Traditional** approach to social transactions creates **social equality** while encouraging **courteous behavior** producing **positive outcomes** for all actors.

Actor 2 says, "please" as not to demean Actor 1 who is obligated to satisfy Actor 2's request. "Please" balances the transaction.

Actor 2 says, "thank you" after Actor 1 fulfills their request to dismiss the perception of a subservient relationship. Thank you balances the transaction.

Actor 1 says, "you're welcome" expressing appreciation for the transaction.

The transaction ends **balanced**.

The **Modern** approach to social transactions creates **social inequality** while encouraging **discourteous behavior** producing **negative outcomes**.

The Modern approach ends with an unbalanced transaction when Actor 1 says "No problem" indicating to Actor 2 that they shouldn't feel too much like a jerk for bothering Actor 1. Modern Actor 1's paradigm is they're just hanging-out putting their time in when Actor 2 shows-up wanting something from them. Actor 1 ends the transaction by saying "no problem" indicating to Actor 2 that they appreciate their not being a pain in the ass by asking too much. It makes little difference in this paradigm whether Actor 1 is being compensated for or is volunteering their time.

The transaction ends **unbalanced**.

Why You Should Say Thank You
Saying "you're welcome" ends in a balanced transaction.

Saying "no problem" ends in an unbalanced transaction.

Balanced transactions support equitable civil societies whereas unbalanced transactions support exploitive uncivil societies.

Don't underestimate the importance of courtesy in maintaining civil societies.

Say, "You're welcome".

Why American Men Will Never Like Soccer

There's no scoreboard.

Game time counts up to the end of a game not down forcing you to calculate the mathematical formula:

$$(RT\text{-}CT) + {}^{\sigma_x \sigma_p \geq} \frac{\hbar}{2}, = TR + AT = ATR$$

where RT is Regulation Time, CT is Current Time, followed by Heisenberg's http://en.wikipedia.org/wiki/Werner_Heisenberg

Uncertainty Principle
http://en.wikipedia.org/wiki/Uncertainty_principle

where TR is Time Remaining, AT Added time (Will be discussed later.) and ATR is Actual Time Remaining every time you want to know how much time is left and that's assuming you're smart and/or sober enough to do the calculation. By the time you've figured out Actual Time Remaining (ATR) time has past making your answer obsolete and that's not taking into account the effect on ATR of the Theory of Relativity http://en.wikipedia.org/wiki/Theory_of_relativity. It's a mess.

When it's time to start the players saunter onto the field holding the hands of little boys.

In My Time

Player's experience an existential threat upon any amount of aggressive physical contact or even strongly articulated words of disfavor.

What little hitting there is causes players to roll around on the ground, cry, clutch their teammates, scream-out their last Will and Testament, faint, require immediate medical attention, a stretcher, and much consoling by their teammates, coaches, trainers, and fans. Fortunately, all of them make miraculous recoveries within seconds.

Some players wear colored stretchy bands around their heads to keep their hair out of their eyes. It something chicks do.

Cheerleaders are shown rarely if ever.

Low scores.

A lot of boring time watching players kick a weird-colored ball around.

Slow motion makes players look even more effeminate.

Pastel colored uniforms that are so garishly stylish only wives or girlfriends would make you wear them to warn other woman that you're not only taken you're also severely whipped.

Can't use your hands however you can use your head but that's only to "head" the ball. Can't do *WWF* type head-butts, which would make soccer ever so slightly more interesting.

A lot of time wasted adjudicating penalties.

Even more time is wasted after a penalty has been assessed because referees have to argue with what looks like enraged little girl gangs.

Too much time wasted on fake injuries.

In My Time

When there is a fight, which is extremely rare, they slap and push each other and scream and cry. Although these catfights miffs and tussles participants they never produce battle wounds thus there is no honor.

Players act snippy to their opponents, teammates, trainers, and referees.

Not nearly enough hot woman shown gratuitously.

No beer commercials with hot women.

No grilling commercials with hot women.

No shaving commercials with hot women.

No hardware commercials with hot women.

No car parts commercials with hot women.

No car commercials with hot women.

No "The Most Interesting Man in the World" http://en.wikipedia.org/wiki/The_Most_Interesting_Man_in_th e_World commercials.

Not enough brakes in the game to allow for peeing, eating, and settling back in comfy chair before play resumes.

For some reason they add different amounts of time AT (See above.) at the end of games so you never know when one will actually end.

Players scream, cry, and run around like little girls when they score.

Not enough white lines on the field.

Players hold their hands-up and look like little bitches when they're trying to act innocent.

In My Time

The balls look and are probably foreign made.

Ball doesn't have the primal look and feel like a football.

Goalies wear gloves.

Players wear shin guards.

The sideline referee wears Go-GO shorts and has a little flag he waves for some reason.

The bench areas look like VIP Lounges in high-end strip-clubs. (I have no problem with that I'm just mentioning it because it's a very astute observation.)

For some reason one-side lines up in front of the goal and a player from the opposing team kicks a ball at them. The players who are lined-up hold their hands over their testicles because they aren't men enough to take a hit in the junk for the team.

No spit, puke, blood, Gatorade or any combination there of.

Cheering is weird because fans blow horns, sing foreign sounding songs, and riot.

Names of teams sound foreign.

To Europeanish.

Women and Water

A 72-year-old friend of mine was very upset because his water bill had increased over 20% (about $3.00 more per month) in just one year even though he hadn't increased his water usage. He asked his Apartment Manager why his bill had increased so much and was told that she didn't know because a contractor did all of their billing.

By the way, he's a conspiracy addict. He'd never let even the hint of a conspiracy go unexploited. He has to have a least three conspiracies going on or he feels sad and listless. The research, study, discussion, and exposing of conspiracies gives meaning to his life.

My friend imagined a scheme where San Antonio Water System (SAWS) were increasing clandestinely water rates using the stolen money to fund nefarious activities having to do with keeping SAWS protected from oversight by red-blooded Americans thus giving them a free-hand to snuff out any opposition to their secret One World Order plans. I know it rambles and sounds crazy but doesn't it sound like most other conspiracy theories?

As Founder of the SAWS conspiracy theory he was obligated to ensure it didn't ride the Crazy Train to Crazy Town and disappear. No sir. He swore he'd spend as much time and money as it'd take to expose SAWS. He imagined he'd receive numerous accolades from conspiracy fringe groups who, like him, live in Crazy Town. He imagined his future filled with interviews, speeches, consulting gigs, etc. and becoming the go-to guy for analysis and commentary on all things conspiracy. With this in mind he drove to SAWS Headquarters, went inside, walked up to a clerk who was sheltered prudently behind a crazy-proof window and demanded three years of records for the apartment building he lived in. The clerk told him that she couldn't give him the records because he wasn't the owner of the property. Well that sealed it Buddy. He knew he was onto something. He tried not to get upset with the clerk because he knew she was just a stooge. He asked her again for the records and she again told him she couldn't give them to him. She also signaled to the security guard that she was dealing with one of SAWS's residents of Crazy Town. Apparently, most public agencies have their own dedicated residents of Crazy Town who will periodically stop by to demonstrate just how crazy they really are. No one said democracy was easy.

Being denied the information he thought he had a right too but didn't and being watched closely by security guards until he left the parking lot were clues leading to the only conclusions possible; he was onto a huge insidious scam involving hundreds of people and millions of dollars, and he'd have to be security conscious for the rest of his life. He'd be a wanted man. He became really paranoid knowing that hit men in black outfits and masks were going to kick his door in some night and put a bullet into his head. It was about this time we met to catch-up on our thoughts and writing.

He updated me on the "One World", "Bit Burger", and "Alien Abduction" conspiracies finally mentioning his own conspiracy called "The SAWS Secret Price Increase Conspiracy". He whispered to me that he was hot on the trail of something that's going to blow something wide-open. I asked for more details. He told me he'd discovered his water bill went up over 20% in a year and when he tried to find out why he was stoned-walled by his Apartment Manager and a SAWS stooge clerk who were obviously covering for very powerful players.

In My Time

I really hated to break his heart. I know how much he enjoys conspiracies that can never be proven. Especially theories seasoned with paranoia and fantasy danger like you see in movies involving people who have to be snuffed because they know too much for their own good. He was so excited.

I asked him if his water was billed on an "allocated" basis. He said, "Yeah".

I asked him if there were more women living in his apartment building now than before his water bill increase. He said, "Yeah there's more women so what?"

I told him an "allocated basis" means that the total monthly water usage of all residents of the building is divided by the number of bedrooms in the building. If you have a one-bedroom apartment you pay for one unit of the allocated costs. If you have three bedrooms you pay for three units of the allocated costs. The reason his water bill increased is because per capita women use significantly more water than men. A three bedroom apartment with three woman will use at least three times more water than an apartment with three men.

The reasons why women use significantly more water than men are numerous and varied having to do with women insisting on taking too long and too many showers; having a higher standard of cleanliness than men in every area to include clothes, bedding, bathrooms, floors, walls, ceilings, counters, dishes, pots and pans, refrigerators, etc.; the pathological need to wash and reuse dishes and utensils rather than using disposable plastic dishes and sporks; and being diligent, bordering on obsessive, in keeping their genetic heritage (kids) and all that comes with them i.e. diapers, toys, bedding, clothes, etc. clean. It goes on and on.

Women are complex creatures whose existence ripples through our lives. Unfortunately, women my friend barely knew drove him temporarily insane. But that's nothing new. Women have been driving men crazy since the beginning of time. Didn't Eve drive Adam so crazy that he finally ate the apple?

In My Time

You're Not That Fascinating

I've suffered through many years of people feeling manically compelled to tell me every single detail of their rather mundane existence. They clearly think they're fascinating and want to share their fascination. After suffering literally thousands of hours of being the recipient of others verbal catharsis I've discovered a few Truths.

While growing up they were told they were very special, unique, and no one was just like them. This is true in theory but it leads to the mistaken belief that they're "specialness" and "uniqueness" makes them fascinating.

They're not very intelligent making their life very challenging. Simple social transactions seem complicated making them feel compelled to share with you every single detail of how they overcome some perceived "challenge" thinking you'll be just as amazed as they are by their success.

Life confuses them so they have to talk things out to try to understand what's going on. (Ref: Not very intelligent comment above.)

They're starved for meaningful relationships so they force you to listen to them simulating a genuinely caring relationship.

They want to impress you with their daring-do exploits.

In My Time

They're narcissistic.

They're ill mannered.

They're passive aggressive.

They have low self-esteem.

They're hoped-up on drugs or caffeine or both.

They love their family and friends so much they feel compelled to tell you about them.

They re-experience good memories by talking about them.

They enjoy life so much they just have to share there's with you.

They're just messing with you.

You're boring.

I think it is a generational paradigm because it seems the older the person is the more likely it is to have a mutually satisfying and respectful conversation. Talking at each other is very prevalent in younger generations because they were raised on the mantra that they're so special, they're so unique, and there's no one just like them. Unfortunately, this causes a verbal traffic jam with younger people because each one is only suffering the other person talking long enough for them to brake in and start they're own equally boring story.

A symptom of each person thinking they're fascinating is evidenced when a group of young people are sitting together staring down at their telephones texting and surfing the Internet rather than talking to each other. I've seen young people sitting at the same table texting each other rather than raising their heads and talking. I think there are two reasons they do this. First of all, no one is listening to them making them feel unappreciated so they ignore each other. Second, there's too much competition within the group to tell fascinating stories causing stress. They relieve this stress by not competing.

I've always thought you should listen more then you talk because that's how you learn about people and places. It's impossible to listen if you're talking and since you already know so much about yourselves you should take the opportunity to learn about someone else.

Finally, truly pathologically fascinating people will read this essay and think it describes everyone else.

In My Time

American Women Have Gotten Hotter

A men's antiperspirant commercial on T. V. reminded me of an idea I had a few years ago. The gist of the commercial was that women are getting hotter so men had better use their product to stay in the game.

I'm a voracious and eclectic reader who's read literally thousands of books with the majority being non-fiction history. Many times I'd read about a woman who was considered a "rare beauty" by her contemporaries with many men lined-up to court her. I'm always disappointed when I see a picture of the "rare beauty" because she always looks frumpy, much older than her age, and not like she'd be cool to party with at all.

Thesis Summary

Thesis: American Women Have Gotten Hotter

Women's hotness increased significantly in the 50s. This was a time when women started receiving better healthcare, food, and a plethora of appliances were becoming available to reduce the drudgery of housework. These three factors combined to limit the forces negatively effecting hotness. For the first time in history hotness had the time and resources to increase its genetic expression within the America population.

American women's hotness continued increasing through the 70s with a major tipping point marked by Farrah Fawcett's 1976 bathing suit poster that broke sales records with over 20 million copies sold. From that point on women's hotness increased substantially while expanding into newly discovered ethnic hotness.

The Hotness Virtuous Cycle

American women's hotness is driven ever higher via a Virtuous Cycle where hotter women have more mates to choose from than lesser hot women. Increased mate selection increases the chances that hotties, being typical women, will select mates with money rather then good looks thus producing hot daughters who grow up to be hotter than their mothers who produce even hotter daughters. Around and up goes the Cycle driving us to the situation we have today.

Men have stayed pretty much the same over the years, give or take whiskers, and since women are biased towards money rather then good looks men's physical evolution has stalled. Unfortunately, it will take centuries for men to catch up to women if we ever can.

The best strategy for men to cope with the hotness imbalance is to believe in and propagate "The Great Delusion". The Great Delusion makes men believe that it's entirely possible for a 53-year-old gray-haired short fat bald guy to date a 21 year old making her ecstatically happy without spending a boatload of cash. This Delusion also helps men enjoy the unrequited hotness of woman without experiencing any guilt whatsoever. The Great Delusion is also evident when men look in the mirror and see hotness where there is none.

Future Research

My fervent hope is that my research raises awareness of the pervasive hotness disparity between men and women in American while stimulating additional research and efforts to increase said disparity. As a professional I'm dedicated to research and will continue my quest for knowledge by visiting as many Hooters possible.

May God continue to bless America.

An Adirondack Trail in the Fall

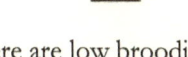

There are low brooding skies
hanging dark and heavy

you're wearing an old battered hat and soft clothes
shielding you from crisp mulchy air

your heavy boots are crunching blazing colors carpeting the trail
that is curving bending-up around down and into the gray mist

you see tough trees surviving years of harsh weather
enclosing the trail like soft living walls

you have fond memories of traveling
with lost family and friends

you hear quiet sounds muffled off in the distance
making you feel primal loneliness

but you're comforted knowing
that bitch Lady Nature is finally at rest.

In My Time

Because the Absence of Pain Isn't Felt

Because the absence of pain isn't felt:

painful feelings fad slowly over time.

it's very difficult to empathize with someone in pain.

people do really stupid things injuring or killing themselves and/or others.

we can watch horrible things done to innocent people in movies and call it entertainment.

you committed yourself to something before you knew what it'd entail which is good because if you had known you wouldn't have done it thereby achieving nothing.

we're much more willing to take a shot of cheap whiskey before taking the shot rather than after taking the shot.

when one of your Jabrounee friends yells, "Hey. Watch this!" you stand and watch rather than hauling-ass far away to safety.

you do stupid things when you're drunk like eating Ghost chilies while taking shots of cheap Tequila.

you put-off a whole lot of stuff you should do but don't.

government leaders resists changes that doesn't benefit them directly or weakens their power.

you always choose beautiful women with bad characters.

Adam and Eve ate the apple.

people smoke cigarettes underestimating cancer.

you repeat mistakes because you don't remember their painful consequences.

some people create drama because they can't live a painless life.

you let things happen because others (not you) feel the painful consequences.

Communities of Unreality

Over the last twenty years people have become much more emotional while discussing their ideas and are significantly more entrenched in their thinking. Most people live a comfortable existence in a world they've constructed whose paradigm is a positive feedback loop that reinforces their thinking rather then challenging and improving their mind. Their positive feedback loop is created specifically to reinforce their thinking while considering opposing ideas as existential threats. The information they choose to attend too reinforces their thinking while excluding opposing ideas.

When I was in undergraduate and graduate schools opposing views were routinely studied and debated. We valued opportunities to learn what other people thought because we wanted to improve our minds. We searched for alternative views appreciating others who didn't agree with us because they provided us with an opportunity to learn.

The Internet was supposed to allow people from all walks of life to access the ideas of others thus making the world a better place. Unfortunately, an unintended consequence of the Internet is that instead of seeking alternative views people are accessing information that agrees with what they already think. This situation creates Communities of Unreality where people form self-referencing communities clustered around ideas they think are the Truth compelling them to defend their ideas with as much dedication and veracity as a tribe would have in defending their land.

Communities of Unreality

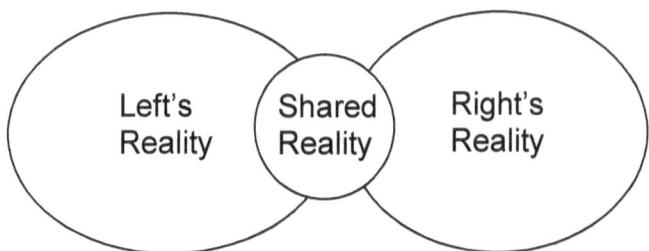

The above diagram depicts three realities:

- The Left's Reality is centered on being "good", "caring", "nice", "accepting", "tolerant", "just", etc.
  - They describe the Right's Reality as "mean-spirited", "homophobic", "moralistic", "intolerant", "prejudice", etc.

- The Right's Reality is centered on "personal responsibility", "capitalism", "morality", etc.
  - They describe the Left's Reality as "socialistic", "unrealistic", "nannyish", etc.

- Shared Reality is the realm of ideas that the Left and Right have in common and is the area that has shrunk significantly over the last twenty years.

The Gestalt of a Community of Unreality is the cluster of ideas that make-up the Community. Joining groups that agree with what you think creates a self-referencing Community that reinforces their ideas through newsletters, blogs, literature, etc. Since you've limited yourself to receiving only positive information about your idea you don't know that there may be opposing views.

In My Time

I think this is why "scream fests" have become the standard. A media producer will seek out people with opposing realities than turn them lose on each other knowing the conflict will make for an exciting show even though civility is sacrificed and there is no increase in knowledge.

There must be bridges between the three realities, Left, Right, and Shared or our country will continue down the Jerry Springer road where people yell at each other rather than exchanging ideas. If we don't build bridges between the Realities or country may end-up being so fractured that it will become ungovernable or destroyed.

In My Time

A Fall Day

The soft feeling of leafs returning to the cold dead ground.

Crisp clean air smelling of vegetation decaying into the Earth.

The Sky dark and brooding waiting its time to Rein.

Ominous grey clouds overhead warning of cold snowy months ahead.

Leafs hanging dead in their colorful glory waiting for Mother Nature to complete their Cycle of Life. Longing to return to Earth where they came.

A deeply pleasant anticipation of months of cold and snowy weather ahead challenging your Spirit.

Looking forward to precious time spent with family and friends bundled in warm homes with frosty windows on the outside and dewy windows on the inside evidence of sumptuous meals being prepared. Dinners prepared by the Woman in your life who feels a satisfying need to serve you while you watch hours and hours of FOOTBALL. A time when you and your Woman enjoy spending time together yet comfortably apart.

In My Time

Fall reminds me of Football games played in the high school stadium near my childhood home in Northeast New York. I remember hearing the sounds of bands playing and the gentle roar of the crowd flowing into the chilly clear night to me in my backyard. I didn't know that in the years ahead I'd play on the same field creating sounds for the next generation to hear.

Fall is a Man's Season. It's when football, hunting, and Mother Nature combine challenging Men to live. It's when our necks swell, our muscles seem to be harder, and we fell GOOD! Damned GOOD! It's when the Woman in our life look especially fetching.

Fall is when the chaos of the year ends and a more introspective and restful time begins.

Falls the time of year to slow-down and be proud of your accomplishments and plan for new challenges in the year ahead. A time when you fix your life in time and come to understand how you're living it.

Fall is when the furious activities of survival take a time out. It's when what's happened has happened and you are consoled to the outcome.

It took many years to know why I loved the Fall. After years of thought I learned Fall represents death. Death is required for life to renew in the Spring. Without Death, there is no new life.

Men are animals. Our brain knows we are; it's our minds and society that denies it.

If we would listen to our brains we'd slow-down, feast, drink, make babies, and look forward to restful months of quiet thought. The year's harvest is in; we should enjoy the rewards.

Most Men continue to do what they do all year filling Fall with mindless activities taking short impotent pauses on holidays to reminisce but not to Think.

In My Time

This Fall make a promise to yourself that you'll stop and spend time to understand who you are as a Man and who you want to become.

Do it for yourself and, more importantly, do it for your Family.

In My Time

God's Little Jokes

God, among other things, has an excellent sense of humor and since He's our Creator His jokes are the funniest and most profound. He made us so He knows what makes us laugh.

I went to church to attend a presentation on Science and Faith. I had a cup of Starbucks coffee, climbed up to the high mezzanine level with only one row behind me than you hit a wall. I ascended to those heights because I wanted to be alone and relax and concentrate on the presentation. So I just settled in when I spied a Mommy climbing the stairs carrying one kid with two in tow. I comforted myself thinking that she couldn't climb all the way up to me with all those kids. But she did. Yupper. I guess she's one of them aerobic Stairmaster type Moms. No one within 30 feet of me yet they invade the last row right behind mine.

I was miffed because I knew the brats would be noisy and Mommy'd be Mommy and my night was ruined.

As I was stewing over the above I looked down and saw ANOTHER Mommy climbing the stairs with two kids. They climbed ALL THE WAY up the stairs and installed themselves in the row right in front of me. Yupper. So picture this, I climb all the way to the top of the place to get away from people yet there I sit sandwiched between two Mommies and five kids and with no one else within thirty feet of us. I grew even more miffed.

In My Time

Sometime after the second Mommy and kids landed I thought about what happened and laughed. The Mommies and kids were quiet and it was nice to have company so what I knew would be an uncomfortable situation ended-up being pleasant. God sent the first Mommy and kids up to mess with me. When I didn't see the humor God sent the second Mommy and kids. It was then that I saw the humor.

I swear to you that what is written below is the Truth

Just when I started writing the first paragraph of this fascinating study of God's humor four middle-aged ladies who hadn't talked to each other in a while set-up camp in the four chairs immediately to my right. These ladies were talking about weddings, health, relationships, kids, husbands, food, vacations, weather, ad nauseam and with absolutely no remorse. (For additional information read my article on What A Woman Needs) Before they intruded I was sitting alone in perfect public/private bliss. However, I'm now compelled to hear their extremely psychologically painful conversation that will leave permanent and deep scars on my psyche.

Think about it. God's playing another joke on me while I'm writing about a joke He played on me before!

God created the three-part structure of a traditional joke. The first part establishes the situation, the second reinforces the situation, and the third is the punch line. In this joke my writing about the two Mommies and their kids establishes the situation, the ladies babbling away next to me reinforces the situation having to do with the invasion of my privacy, and the punch line is that I shouldn't take life to seriously because if I do He'll keep messing with me until I live La Dolce Vita. God's little jokes are analogies instructing us on how to live life. He'll keep sending them to us until we change. He'll never quit on us.

They don't call Him the Master for nothing.

Even more intriguing after finishing the above I got in line to get a coffee refill. There was a Mommy and her two cheerleader daughters holding-up the line for over five minutes discussing the situation and other gossipy observations, debating their choices of drinks and snacks, who should get what so others can taste it, than after an elaborate order was placed Mommy paid and the show moved down the line. Immediately behind them and in front of me was a rough looking Man wearing a black leather jacket. After the Mommy and daughters exited stage left he turned to me and laughed. I couldn't help myself and started laughing. We didn't have to say anything. We both got the humor of how ironic it was that the Mommy and girls were holding us Men up acting like females without having a clue about what they were doing to others thus encroaching in our lives and their wasn't a damned thing we could do about it. So we laughed.

…and His jokes keep coming.

In My Time

How Dads Are

I was at a Barbeque restaurant where you moved along a steam table line making your choices stopping at the end where the cashier waited. While standing in line I couldn't help notice the behavior of the family in front of me. There was a Dad, Mom, Son, and Daughter.

I noticed Son and Daughter, who were in there early teens, were having a disagreement. Son kept bugging his Sister by draping his arm over her shoulders and leaning on her. The Son v Daughter battle went on until it was Daughter's turn to order. Daughter shrugged her Brother's arm off her shoulders, gave him a LOOK, and ordered. Apparently, the LOOK was the signal for Brother to cut the crap so he did. Brother followed Daughter down the line.

Mother (The Cradle of Civilization) followed Daughter and Brother down the line. Mother ordered for herself while changing Daughter and Brother's selections to more healthy alternatives. Mom monitored the internal activities of her family while Dad kept an eye-out for external threats.

Dad was in front of me holding down the family's anchor position. He placed his order while herding his family down the line past the cashier. Daughter, Son, and Mom passed by the cashier without hesitating because they knew Dad was behind them and would take care of everything. The family set-up a noisy camp at a table in the center of the restaurant.

It made me think of an old joke where slapstick comics would rush through a cafeteria line. When they got to the cashier they'd indicate that the guy behind them was going to pay. The last guy would try the same thing but since there was no one behind him he had to pay for everyone. Like I said it's and old joke.

I asked Dad, "Wouldn't you know it? You're the last guy in line."

Dad turned to me whispered, "Yeah but I'm blessed to have a family to pay for and the ability to do it."

After paying Dad sat down with his family without being acknowledged. He was absorbed into the their family circle without even a thought.

That's how Dad's are.

How to Survive Life

When I was a boy I'd watch my Grandfather enjoying himself while sitting quietly on his front porch. I couldn't understand how he could just sit for hours on end sedately watching the world pass him by. It wasn't until I reached 50 years old that I began to understand my Grandfather.

He was a wise Old Man.

One day I was driving minding my own business when I heard on the radio that malaria was making a big come back in Vietnam. The reporter told me that I should be very concerned about it. Normally, my first reaction was to be concerned followed by making a mental note to monitor the malaria situation in a third-world county I had zero chance of visiting located on the other side of the planet.

This is when I had one of my many epiphanies. I thought why and hell do I care about malaria in Vietnam and why is their an expectation that I should? Why should I spend even one pico (one trillionth or 10-12) second of my life worrying about something that had no effect on me whatsoever? I tired to care about malaria in Vietnam but I just couldn't. Like my Grandfather I learned that I needn't care about malaria in Vietnam because I'm a Survivor.

In My Time

Up to this writing I've survived global warming and cooling;
nuclear arms race; the Cold War; acid rain; AID's; asbestos; lead
in paint and drinking water; flesh eating bacteria; Ebola; Swine
and Bird flues; antibiotic resistant TB and assorted other
microbes; PCBs; Styrofoam; mercury in water and fish; recession;
inflation; stagflation; hyper-growth of the economy; meltdowns
on Wall Street; bankruptcy of multi-national corporations; the
credit crunch; high and low interest rates; the changing value of
the dollar; foreigners buying U.S. real estate; the depletion of the
Rainforest; Y2K; the potential for asteroids and space junk
destroying the earth; black holes; exploding white dwarfs;
something called singularity; the threat of the sun burning itself
out billions of years in the future; the retraction of the universe
billions of years from now; just all-around unsafe drinking water;
ever larger carbon footprints; increasing UV rays and Co2 in the
atmosphere; a dearth of vitamin D for some reason I can't
remember; prostate and frequent urination problems; impotency;
hair loss; the heartbreak of psoriasis; hemorrhoids; athlete's foot;
dandruff; diabetes; alcoholism; the suffering of a variety of
downtrodden populations; over and under population; deadly
sexually transmitted diseases; heart attacks and strokes; cancer;
everyone's obesity including my own; violent death; kidnapping;
gun violence; drug addiction; drive-by shootings; serial murderers;
pedophiles lurking in my neighborhood; meth labs; crack-heads;
heroin addicts who would kill me for a couple of bucks to "get a
fix"; unsafe tires; sitting to close to the TV; the deadly
consequences of breathing various invisible fumes emanating
from a variety of materials; consuming non-organic food; eating
too much or too little fat and protein; floods; droughts;
earthquakes; killer bees, ants, and other vermin poised to kill or
severely maim me; being raised in a patriarchal society; dirty
bombs; anthrax in the mail; measles; mumps; diphtheria; decaying
teeth; no seatbelts or air bags; methane gas from animal dung; not
composting; corn syrup...

When I was a high school freshman in 1975 we were taught the
earth's atmosphere was cooling because something up in the sky
was reflecting the suns rays. (I don't remember what that
something was but it shouldn't be their and it was our fault.) The
blocking of the suns rays was causing the earth to cool-down

In My Time

increasing the amount and distribution of snow and ice. This caused an irreversible chain reaction of more snow and ice reflecting more of the suns rays causing the earth to cool-down even more thus producing more snow and ice. (Read it a couple of times it'll make sense.)

We were warned the earth was undergoing a downward spiral of cooling temperatures that would usher in a new Ice Age. We were told glaciers would grow out of Canada, engulf the Great Lakes, and cover the earth with ice and snow as far southern Pennsylvania. Because of decreasing temperatures and a whole lot more snow and ice humans would become shorter and grow more hair to conserve heat.

Now a mere 35 years later, practically no earth time, I'm told the earth is warming and I should be very very concerned about it. But as much as I've tried I just can't get concerned about global warming because I suspect it's just a normal weather cycle and very shortly we'll be told the earth's temperature is leveling off followed by its cooling again.

I think I've burned-out the part of my brain where concern is generated and stored.
Well anyways back to why my Grandfather was a wise Old Man.

Anyone who's survived as long as my Grandfather learned to discern what's important and should be attended to and what is not. Being young and dumb I never appreciated the years of living it took for my Grandfather to earn the peace of mind to sit on his porch and enjoy watching the world pass him by. Now I look forward to my grandchildren looking at me wondering how I can just sit there.

In My Time

Man Up

I was in Starbucks minding my own bidness when I overheard a conversation between a pretty young lady and a mitch (male who is a bitch). They were sitting next to each other studying for a high school psychology test.

The mitch was skinny, pale, and expressed his feelings freely.

The young lady mentioned she was mad at her boyfriend. The mitch asked if she wanted to talk about it. She said no.

The mitch asked the young lady if here hair color was natural. The young lady said yes.

The mitch told her that he broke up with his girlfriend because she was cheating on him the entire time. The young lady was non-committal.

The mitch told the young lady that he was going to "hit the gym" again with his friend who is a "Holston (sic?) model". He said his friend was getting really muscular, "he's a monster". The young lady was unimpressed. The mitch kept talking about his friend's body.

The mitch tried to get the young lady to sing something with him. She declined.

In My Time

The mitch talked about a party someone was having. He expressed how upset he'd be if he weren't invited.

Throughout their conversation the mitch provided deeply felt feedback on how she was reacting to what he was saying. He'd say, "You're eyes got big when I said that. Why?" She and I were getting annoyed.

God made male and female similar so that we can have a relationship but different enough to make things interesting. The male is stall word the female is emotional. It balances out. It's not emotionally satisfying when men and woman act the same. I for one declare, "Long live the difference! (vive la difference)".

Mayberry Wisdom

Barney was at the Courthouse/Jail looking through old files when he found a thirty-year-old assault case that was still open involving Floyd the barber. Barney thought it was his duty to investigate the case so it could be closed properly. Andy kept telling Barney to stop what he's doing and forget about the case. Barney refused to drop the case because he said it was his duty to perform a complete investigation. Barney ends up causing a whole lot of trouble because Floyd and Walt (the guy Floyd allegedly assaulted) start another fight over the details, etc. of the fight thirty years previous.

Scene: Andy is sitting in Floyds barber chair getting a haircut. Barney just left the barbershop really motivated and pissed-off because he's getting stonewalled by Andy and Floyd. Barney had just finished interrogating Floyd about the assault case when he left. There is a pause after Barney storms out then Floyd says:

> "You know the problem with him?
> He's not married.
> If he were none of these little problems would bother him."

In My Time

Mansplaining

Definition:

Mansplaining ['mansplayning]

n

Speech unique to men

[from Greek, *aner* man - + - from English male genre, *splayning* explaining,]

mansplainer *n & adj*

mansplaynorous *adj*

Mancode English Dictionary – Complete and Unabridged, 2003.

Mansplaining occurs when men purposely misuse words to explain/translate/exaggerate phenomena. The following are examples, excluding exhaustive derivations, of mansplaining using the Olde English word "ton" meaning weighting 2,000 pounds:

He was told tons of times.
He's done it a ton of times.
I've seen it a ton of times.
There's tons of reasons.
He got a ton of yards.
He scored a ton of points.
He's got tons of speed.

He had tons of time.
He can eat tons.
She must weigh a ton.
This weighs a ton.
It felt like a ton.
I got tons of emails.
I've got a ton of work to do.

In My Time

I ate a ton.	He's made a ton of movies.
I could eat a ton.	I ran a ton of miles.
It cost a ton of money.	Give me a ton of it.
I drove it a ton of times.	He hit it a ton.
I did it a ton of times.	It went a ton of miles.
There's tons of space.	It should've gone tons of miles.
He hit me like a ton of bricks.	He's hit it a ton farther.
I hit him like a ton of bricks.	Etc.

As of this writing mansplaining misusing "ton" is still spoken almost exclusively by males. However, there is growing concern that "ton" will go the way of "dude" which was also spoken almost exclusively by males until female hip-hoppers started using "dude(s)". Shortly thereafter "dude" hit the mainstream losing its coolness for the foreseeable future. I hope "ton" will remain exclusively male because it's unladylike for women to call anyone "dude" just as it's unladylike for them to speak unsymantically.

Men Caught in the Middle

There's an ancient story about a monk who's standing at the edge of a cliff looking out over a beautiful valley.

He hears a rustling noise behind him. He turns around to see a huge Tiger stalking him from a clump of bushes. He sees the Tiger is famished and he's its prey.

The monk looks over the edge of the cliff seeing a single branch sticking out.

He climbs over the edge of the cliff and hangs by the branch. He thinks he can hang there until the Tiger leaves.

He looks-up at the edge of the cliff and sees the Tiger peering down at him. The Tiger isn't moving.

The monk looks down the wall of the cliff thinking he can drop-down and run-away.

He sees another famished Tiger looking up at him waiting for him to fall.

The monk is stuck between two horrible alternatives.

In My Time

The monk looks over and sees a little bush clinging to the side of the cliff. Growing out of it is the most beautiful strawberry he's ever seen.

He reaches over and picks the strawberry.

He bites into the strawberry. It tastes better than anything he's ever eaten.

He takes his time eating the strawberry completely forgetting his circumstances.

What does this story mean to Men?

The Tigers are the forces around us devouring our desire to be fulfilled.

Hanging on the cliff is our precarious position in society.

The branch is other Men who support us keeping us alive and thriving.

Eating the strawberry is the moments in our life when we ignore what's going-on around us and enjoy living in the present.

Find the strawberries in your life and eat as many as you can.

Men, Women, and Golf

Over the last 3+ years I've lived in a Townhouse next to the 17th Green and the 18th Tee Box of a public golf course. Over the years I've observed a large number of people playing golf noting that there are significant differences in the Gestalt of a group that is dependant on the gender makeup of said group.

For instance, when a woman only group plays the Gestalt is kindness, support, and encouragement with comments such as: "Great shot!", "Oh thank you so much"; "You go girl!" (The "girl" in question shot a 10 on a par 3.); "Oh that swing doesn't count"; "Good try!"; "Wow you're doing great!"; etc.

When a group is made up of men and woman the Gestalt is kindness, support, and encouragement with low-level competition. I've heard comments such as: "Good shot. To bad you're still out"; man says to a woman "Good drive. Almost as far as mine." (A double dig because woman's tees are closer to the hole.); "Tough course for you huh?"; "You'll do better next time."; etc.

After inexpertly analyzing data from my wholly unscientific study I've concluded the optimum makeup of a group is all male. By optimum group I mean the group with a Gestalt best suited to enjoying fully the game of golf. I've discovered this after hearing the following comments: "Well your shot sucked."; "Ha, ha, ha, dip shit you missed." (Said while jumping up and down and pumping fists.)"; "You're going to shank it."; "Man you hit like a girl."; "Don't blame it on the club. It's the little girl behind the club."; "You can't putt for shit."; "You couldn't make that shot to save your wasted worthless life."; "You're a pussy."; "Good thing you don't do this for a living."; "Even if I did put hair around it you couldn't sink it."; "I hope you **** better than you putt."; "Watcha' shoot dickhead?"; "You-are-a-piece-of-shit."; "You're completely hopeless."; "After that shot you need to walk some you pissant."(Yelled over his shoulder while driving off with the cart.); "Screw-you."; "Really? Really? Are you really that frickin stupid?"; etc.

After 3+ years I've concluded, and I'm sure you'll agree, that the group Gestalt that provides the most enjoyment of the game is male only.

Stay Awesome Men.

Men's Wallets

I know what you're thinking. WALLETS! You mean this dope is writing about WALLETS? I can hear you thinking it right now but please bear with me. You're about to read something very profound. I promise.

Like many men I wake-up in the morning, perform my ablutions, get dressed, stick my wallet in my back right pocket, and head-out to make War.

One day I was jamming my wallet into my pocket when I felt by the heft of it that it had become huge. It was the size of three Texas Toast slices of bread and weighed as much as two bottles of Piel's Real Draft beer. (The little stubby brown bottles that we used to pay $1.99 a six-pack.) I realized it was the first time in over five-years that I evaluated my wallet for its combat effectiveness.

I sat down on my bed and pulled-out a plethora of cards and evaluated each one.

I had my NRA Distinguished membership card that no one had ever asked me for since joining over ten-years ago.

I had my NRA Pistol Instructor and Range Safety Officer cards which I never used because no one ever doubted my word.

In My Time

I had my Disabled American Veteran membership card which I carried in case I had to prove I was a member and to take advantage of discounts and benefits I never use.

I also carried my COSTCO card because I partake frequently in their $1.50 Hebrew National jumbo hotdog and drink deal.

I had my American Automobile Association membership card that was no longer valid but I carried in case my car battery dies. I bought a five-year warranty battery from them that has been working just fine but, one never knows does one?

I had an old rusty paper clip that I used to attach a $5 bill to my Republic of Panama Driver's license. I was stopped frequently by the Panamanian police because I looked to them like a bank on wheels with my United States Army Officer's blue sticker displayed prominently on my windshield. I would hand my license to the police officer who would examine it dutifully and return it to me sans ticket and $5.

I had a Guardian Angel coin stuck down in one of the card slots that was sent to me by some religious organization wanting money. I never sent them any which is probably why the coin never worked.

There were numerous other cards that are so trivial they're not worth mentioning making me wonder why I carried them around for so long.

I decided to carry in my wallet: credit cards, driver's license, Concealed Handgun License, a picture of my beautiful daughter, COSTCO card (Hotdogs remember?), Veteran Administration card, and that's it.

Oh, and by the way. Under no circumstances will I carry a National I.D. card no matter how many laws the federal government passes. They'll have to pry open and jam the card into my cold dead hand as I'm lying over a huge pile of dead One World like government officials. I voluntarily live in Texas so I follow its laws. When I was commissioned I swore an oath to defend the U.S. Constitution NOT the federal government. Let me clarify. Congress can pass as many laws as they want but if there not constitutional than I ignore them based on the X Amendment...

Anyways.

Over the years I carried a variety of cards that were an expression of my identity. As my interests changed I added more and more cards without culling. When I did cull, I discovered that my wallet was half the size and weight it was. My stream-lined wallet was smaller and lighter reducing my combat load significantly.

I recommend that once in a while Men stop and evaluate where they can lighten their combat loads.

You'll be pleasantly surprised how much more lethal you'll feel.

In My Time

Mother Don't Dress Like Your Daughters

In my short-work above titled "American Women Have Gotten Hotter" I proved definitely that for numerous reasons American women have gotten much hotter over the last 50 years whereas American men haven't changed much over the same timeframe. American women have outpaced men in hotness and due to women's mating paradigm a wide hotness gap will exist long into the foreseeable future. I also discussed in the article how mating behavior of hot women produce hot daughters who have even hotter daughters and thus the Hotness Virtuous Cycle goes round and up to even more hotness.

Unfortunately, the Hotness Virtuous Cycle has created social problems never experienced in the history of this great nation. For over a year I've noticed a number of hot mothers wearing short-shorts up to the base of their gluteus maximus (butt) and tight little cleavage baring shirts with white sneakers for the healthy young sexy look. Now I'm not complaining about hot mothers going about being their hot selves however, I do have a complaint when I see hot mothers being hot around their sons.

Most hot daughters think the clothes their hot mothers wear and their behavior are appropriate because they act the same way and wear the same style clothes. However, by nature, daughters lack wisdom and are immature requiring guidance and protection or they'll end-up pregnant, uneducated, and chronically un/underemployed. So we shouldn't rely on the judgment of daughters to guide us in what is appropriate behavior or apparel for mothers or anyone else.

Sons however rarely want to be with their hot mothers because they are males and know what other males are up too.   Sons feel stressed because they know men are checking-out their mothers and what they're thinking and they can't do a damned thing about it.   Whereas mothers and daughters act more interested in shopping and yakking while being oblivious to their surroundings sons are attuned to their surroundings making them frustrated about a situation they are powerless to resolve. Hot mothers and daughters seem to enjoy or ignore the attention of men whereas sons feel mad, stressed, frustrated, and protective. Sons would much rather their mothers dress more appropriately or stay home.

Hot mothers don't make your sons feel bad because they think they're failing to protect you. If you must dress like you're daughters do so sans sons.

Sons need mothers not flirtatious objects of men's' sexual desires.

Payback

The great Sage and Saint Floyd was giving Andy a trim when he says, "Hey Andy did ya' hear Margaret Sue and Johnny are getting married?"

Andy says, "No. Do tell."

Floyd says, "Yup they announced it yesterday in the paper. Ahhhh... I remember when little Johnny used to dip her pigtails in the inkwells and hide her pencils. Oh boy! Now that they're married she's going to make him pay you can believe that."

Andy says, "Yup I expect so."

In My Time

Pregnant Wife

I was sitting minding my own business, as usual, when I saw a man and a very pregnant woman walk in, get their drinks, then she sat a table and he went about ten-feet away and sat in a comfortable chair. His wife, and I know I'm making a risky and assuredly erroneous assumption about their being married, patted the chair next to her at the table indicating that she wanted her husband to sit next to her. Well hubby, who henceforth we'll call Stupid, was dangerously comfortable where he was so he ignored his wife's beckoning. The Mrs. was disappointed.

The Mrs. waited a couple of minutes then looked back over at Stupid and patted the seat again. Stupid stayed planted in his seat and raised his hand indicating to her that he had to make a call. The Mrs. was disappointed again.

After about 10 minutes on his mobile Stupid gets-up, slouches over, and plops down next to where the Mrs. wanted him to sit previously. Unfortunately, the Mrs.'s temperament, which was rather unstable due to hormones etc. related to pregnancy, had changed in the ensuing period. The Mrs. was no longer feeling loving she was feeling maternal. When a woman's maternal instinct kicks-in she'll do anything to protect her babies up to and including "whacking" the child's father if circumstances should warrant.

So Stupid, who is completely unaware of the danger, looks over at the Mrs. and asks her how she's doing.

The Mrs. goes on the offensive complaining about how tired she is, how hot she feels, how her feet and lower back hurt, how she feels a little dehydrated, and how he needs to get her a bottle of cold water. So Stupid gets-up to get the Mrs. her cold water not having any idea that he's her prey and that she's merely toying with him. The retribution hasn't begun in earnest. In fact it's only just begun. The Mrs. is a lioness who wanted to be reassured by her mate but he failed to heed her call so HE SHALL PAY. OH YES. HE SHALL PAY DEARLY.

Stupid stands in line, buys a bottle of water, slouches back to the table, and hands the bottle to the Mrs.

The Mrs. hands the bottle back to Stupid for him to open.

I think it's was when the cap separated from the bottle that Stupid realized he'd made a big mistake, he was in deep trouble, and he was now going to have to tough things out for the foreseeable future.

Stupid hands the now opened bottle back to the Mrs. who takes a very small sip of water that barely whets her delicate lips, recaps the bottle, and slides it into her massive purse.

Stupid asks the Mrs. how she feels now.

The Mrs. says she feels like her energy level is to low and she wants a pastry with a lot of sugar. Stupid gets up again, stands in line, buys the Mrs. a pastry, and delivers it to her waiting hands. The Mrs. inhales the pastry without comment.

Stupid asks the Mrs. how she feels now.

The Mrs. says she feels a little better and they have to get going because the store was closing in a couple of hours. Stupid asks the Mrs. what store. The Mrs. says the crib store and hadn't he'd been listening to her. They're supposed to spend the evening picking out a crib for the baby. Didn't she tell him about it this week?

Stupid is honestly befuddled because it was probably the first time he'd heard about picking out a crib. I think the plan was to get coffee than make their way back home to spend the evening on the couch watching baseball. Well that may have been the initial plan but that plan had changed when Stupid didn't sit with his pregnant wife when she wanted him too.

The Mrs. stands-up like a very pregnant woman would and waddles out the door with Stupid on her left flank. I got the feeling the Mrs. had set the Dogs of War free. Tragically, from that moment on, Stupid will be paying for his failure to heed her call.

In My Time

Send Out Your Women

Nature has left this tincture in the blood,
That all men would be tyrants if they could.
Daniel Defoe (1660-1731)

I want to talk too just the guys here so you ladies stop reading.

Men, I know deep down you want to be a modern day Genghis Khan.

Because if you were you'd lay siege to an area like Los Angeles where's there's a high concentration of Hotties. You'd yell to the Los Anglicans to "**SEND OUT YOUR WOMEN**" because that's the only way you'd lift the siege. The unstated "or else" is that if they don't you'll lead your Armies of World Wrestling Foundation Divas to sack their city and slaughter all of the men. The men will not hesitate to save themselves, being liberal protein and B12 deficient Californians, and will surrender their women without any adieu.

You'd have your throne (Lazyboy) set up in the VIP area of a high-end strip club, with numerous stages, stripper-poles, Thermopedic beds, and giant plasma screens showing ESPN and ESPN2, where exquisitely trained and scantly clad hotties feed you lustfully an unlimited supply of beer, pizza, steaks, chicken wings, and nachos while specially chosen nubile captives perform their most erotic pole dances begging for the privilege of pleasing

In My Time

you. You, being The Great Khan, will choose as many women as you want for your harems with the remainder serving in your Armies, kitchens, pool bars, Formula 1 tracks, putting greens, bowling allies, motocross courses, drag strips, wine cellars, vineyards, distilleries, smoke houses, humidors, yachts, hot springs, and mansions or as members of your Trampoline, Zumba, Aerobic, Cheerleading, Dance or Lingerie Football teams.

Then one day you realize that women are noisy, time-consuming, and expensive and you just can't stand to have so many of them around you. Fortunately, you have a vision of you and ten of your youngest, prettiest, and most pleasantly compliant wives living in a mansion on a hill overlooking the 50-yard line of Notre Dames' football stadium. You tell your oldest son your vision and how he must be the Khan and support you in retirement. Your son agrees because he's young, horny, and isn't sick of having a bunch of women around him yet.

You exit stage left with your ten wives and baggage and are settled into your new mansion long before your other wives even know you're gone so that way you don't have to deal with messy and potentially nasty goodbyes. You end up living a long and happy life producing many manly men and beautiful ladies from your loins with living in Valhalla as your final reward.

All men wish they were Khans.

All right ladies you can stop reading now we're done.

Social Grooming

There's an idea in Social Anthropology that equates Physical Grooming, what monkeys do when they pick lice off each other and eat them, and Social Grooming, what humans do when they embrace and compliment each other. Physical and Social Grooming forms and maintains bonds and structures hierarchal societies.

Humans Socially Groom each other by making pleasant noises and facial expressions, gently touching and rubbing, and making positive comments. The less Social Grooming there is in a relationship the weaker the Social Bond and the more stress due to confusion over their place in the group's Hierarchy.

Women perform Social Grooming much more often and much better than men because they have different genetic goals than men. Women's genetic goal is to limit the gene pool to them and their mate while men's genetic goal is to expand their gene pool to any female.

Women and men's genetic goals differ because of the amount of resources each has to spend conceiving, gestating, birthing, supporting, and teaching a human gambling that they will be viable enough to reproduce the parent's genes. Women have to commit their body, a precious limited supply of ovum, and nine months of pregnancy followed by birth and years of breast-feeding and care. Men commit a relatively short time to the pleasures of mating and an almost unlimited supply of simple celled sperm easily produced almost to the end of life causing them to be less interested in childcare.

Women are more adept at Social Grooming because in an effort to conserve resources they are compelled to rely on their social network of other women to pool resources, share in childcare, seek opinions, and simply talk. I think talking to each other is what women love best. Men are not as attentive to social relationships because, although we require them, we are not as dependent on our social network.

Women are Social Grooming when you hear the following stated enthusiastically:

I love your hair/dress/purse/shoes/ring/bracelet/makeup/eyebrows, etc.

Did you lose weight?

Where'd you get that beautiful tan?

I can't believe you're children are that old.

I can't believe you've had so many children. You don't look it.

Who did your hair/nails/eyebrows/pedicure/wax/facial, etc?

You work so hard you deserve a vacation.

You're mother/father/sister/brother/husband/boyfriend/daughter/son/boss doesn't deserve you.

I miss talking with you.

You're looking good girl.

In My Time

Ad infinitum.

Men are Social Grooming when you hear the following stated lacklusterly:

Hey.
Whatsup?
Whatsup dog?
Grunting sounds.

That's it. We're simple creatures us men.

So the next time you see couples meeting and the women are enthusiastically hugging and talking while the men stand their with their hands in their pockets saying nothing you'll know they're Social Grooming.

In My Time

Teach Our Sons

A while back I was in line at a second-hand bookstore where a mother and her two sons were at the counter. The mother paid for three bags full of books and was having difficulty picking-up the bags to leave the store.

I said, "Excuse me. Are they your sons?"

She said, "Yes."

I looked real hard at the boys and said, "Are you going to let your mother carry those bags?"

The boys looked at me like I had two-heads.

Their mother looked at me with a gleam in her eyes evidence of an epiphany. She turned to her two sons and said, "You're strong. Carry these for me." She looked at me happily and said, "We've never done this before."

I said, "You have boys so they can carry things for you, mow the lawn, sweep the sidewalk..."

The mother, the clerk, and the few people around us laughed.

The mother left the store with her head held high with pride knowing her two sons were in-tow carrying her bags.

In My Time

The mother and boys were very nice people whose paradigm was formed by years of hearing that children are special and fragile beings. The mother, and I assume father, were raising their boys the way modern day experts prescribe thinking they would deform or delay their children's personality development if they burdened their children with non-horizon-expanding activities.

The only lasting effects of children doing chores are pride of accomplishment, feelings of satisfaction in contributing to the family, and many other very positive outcomes.

Chores aren't so bad. Hell, look how well I turned out.

The Player

There was a story in the news about a Player serving a long stretch in a South Carolina prison for numerous willful violations of a variety of Laws beginning when he was very young and continuing on to the present.

While the Player was incarcerated he impregnated four prison guards and used cell phones he had smuggled in to run his gang and very profitable drug bidness. In essence, the Player was doing the same thing he'd done on the street but was doing it within the protective confines of the South Carolina prison system.

The female newscaster was a typical woman misandrist whose reporting was extremely biased against the Player. She was acting like he'd done something wrong. Hell, I think he should be celebrated for being the Alpha Dog of the entire prison including the guards. The Player was thriving in his little area of life where others failed.

The Unholy Trinity of power, money, and sex represented the Player's philosophy of life. You may not agree with the morality of his philosophy but it doesn't mean you can't appreciate the artistry of his devotion and its resulting pleasures.

The Player should be celebrated for thriving in an environment designed to defeat the wills of dangerous criminals.

You can hate the Game but not the Players.

In My Time

The Trouble with Girls

I was at Starbucks the other day minding my own business when a large tribe herded in and set-up camp in the soft chairs right next to where I was sitting. I tried to continue to mind my own business but I couldn't help overhearing their conversations.

They were a mix of three families who were related and hadn't seen each other in years. Someone, most probably a woman, had the idea that the families should meet at a centrally located Starbucks, have coffee, perform tribal Re-bonding Rituals, then continue Re-bonding while attending a dinner theater.

Seemed like a good plan to me however sitting to my left was a dissident sub tribe consisting of a dad looking type guy and three girls who looked and acted like daughters but not sisters. The three daughters ranged from approximately 12-15 years old. Dad just got them their drinks and was sitting down when the daughters started the interrogation. The following is a very inadequate attempt to document the conversation. It's impossible to do justice to the range of emotions the daughters expressed, their verbal mastery, and the impromptu teamwork that developed while interrogating dad.

Daughter 1 (Oldest Daughter) to Dad: When are we going to change?
Dad: Change what?

In My Time

Daughter 1: My clothes.
Dad: Why do you have to change your clothes?
Daughter 1: Because I didn't know we were going to stay out late.
Dad: What does that have to do with it?
Daughter 1: I've just got to change my clothes!
Dad looks off and mumbles something.
Daughter 2 (Middle Daughter): When are we going to eat?
Dad: We're going to have dinner at the dinner theatre.
Daughter 2: Do they have a menu?
Dad: I don't know.
Daughter 2: How are we going to know what's to eat?
Dad: I'm sure they'll tell us.
Daughter 2: What if I don't like anything?
Dad: You will.
Daughter 2 looks very doubtfully at dad but decides to cut him some slack and passes him over to Daughter 3 (The Youngest.)
Daughter 3 to Dad: I have to change my shoes.
Dad: Why?
Daughter 3: Because I don't like them.
Daughter 1 to Dad: Do they know we're coming?
Dad: Yes.
Daughter 1: Who else is going to be there?
Dad: I don't know.
Daughter 3 to Dad: What car am I riding in?
Dad: I don't know we'll figure it out later.
Daughter 1 to Dad: Who has mobiles?
Dad: Why?
Daughter 1: In case we have to call each other on the way.
Dad: Mom's got the numbers.

While dad was being interrogated by one of the daughters the other two carried on spirited side conversations with knowing glances, secret signals, expressions of mutual support, clarifying of ideas, revised strategies for getting out of dad what each one wanted, development of new tactics, all the while rotating interrogating daughters to keep up the pressure and morale.

Dad looked a bit overwhelmed when he jumped up from his seat, walked over to the door, and started to talk with someone. The girls continued to chatter away not deigning to notice that dad had bailed on them. They talked about having to change their clothes, the possibility of not finding anything they wanted to eat, being nervous about who they were going to ride with, etc.

After a short time dad regained his courage and sat back down in his original chair next to the daughters. The daughters started back up again without missing a beat however their new strategy was to move the process along by negotiating a resolution to their demands i.e. change shoes and clothes, food, etc. using their irresistible daughterish charms on poor old dad.

Unfortunately the daughter's efforts came to naught when the matriarchs of the tribe decided they didn't have time to do what the daughters wanted. The daughters surrendered when they heard the decision knowing they were beaten because they couldn't work mom like they could dad. Mom knew all the tricks and couldn't be manipulated.

While all of the above drama was going on with the daughters there was a table of 5 sons ranging in ages from 7 to 13. They were quietly playing a variety of handheld games. The sons didn't say anything to each other except for a grunt now and then when trading games.

Dad looking relieved stood-up and said it was time to go. The tribe stood-up and very noisily herded out the door past the sons.

Dad walked up to sons and said: It's time to go.
The 5 sons stood up and followed the tribe out the door.
One son turned around and asked dad: Where are we going?
Dad: Dinner theatre.
Son: Oh.

Now you know the trouble with girls.

In My Time

They Just Don't Get It

I was talking to a lady friend of mine the other day about a great idea I had. I read just about everything I can get my hands on. Unfortunately this produces a lot of bulky trash consisting of newspapers, magazines, flyers, handouts, etc. I was tired of every two days having to walk all the way out to the dumpster and empty my trashcan. I thought there had to be a better way.

After focusing my massive intellect on the problem I resolved to go to Wal-Mart and buy a big plastic bin to put in my living room next to my chair where I do most of my reading. Wal-Mart has a surprisingly varied selection of inexpensive bins. I choose a big blue one with wheels on one end for easy dragging.

I told the lady since I've had the bin I've only had to empty it once a week. It's been very convenient and a real time saver.

The lady asked, "So in other words you've got a garbage can in your living room?"
I said, "No. It's a bin."
She asked, "Is there garbage in it?"
I said, "Well yes."
She said, "Then it's a garbage can."
I said, "No. It's a bin with wheels for holding discarded papers and such."
She said, "Exactly! A garbage can."

Don't argue with a woman because sometime they just don't get it.

In My Time

Two Young Players

I needed air in my tires so I drove into a gas station, parked, and went in to get change from the cashier.

There was a Hispanic guy at the register. Standing in front of the counter were two young black males all blinged-out like Rap stars. One of them was holding a huge roll of cash of which he pealed-off a couple of bills while his friend next to him did the same. They both dropped a pile of cash on the counter to pay for a Gatorade and a candy bar. We started laughing because they inadvertently way overpaid. I said, "Man the problem with you guys is that you've got to much money." One of them said very respectfully, "Excuse me sir but you can't ever have to much money." Our laugher was interrupted by the second store clerk, a white female, who asked, "Hey you guys like white girls?"

We laughed and the young Players headed out to their car to continue the battle.

In My Time

What a Woman Needs

A woman needs to talk a lot with other women about the drama in their lives.

Reveling in drama is the base of a woman's Pyramid of Hierarchy of Needs. In other words, drama is a primal need that must be met before they can ascend to higher levels of being. Without drama women's lives are dark gray and boring with long lonely days and sad cold nights knowing life is passing them by and they're missing out on something that could complete them and make their life meaningful and worth living but they're frustrated and mad because they don't know what that is and they're driving you and everyone else crazy trying to figure it out.

However, throw a little controlled drama into their life (because if you don't supply the drama they'll generate their own which you will not like it) and have another woman available for them to talk about it and believe me they'll flower. Their and your world will change for the better. This wisdom is written in Man Code Proverbs I : 1, "Happy wife, happy life".

So a woman needs to talk a lot with other women about the drama in their lives.

In My Time

When a Man Gives Up

Men aren't like women. When a man gives up he simply goes about his business of quietly killing himself.
Some men, after reaching a senior age, realize they've lived a full life and the only thing they have to look forward to is a short, painful, declining existence. They realize their body is giving out and they'll never fully enjoy the things they used to do like sex, hunting, fishing, or anything strenuous beyond a slow boring hobbled walk to the mailbox to retrieve the bills and junk mail from the AARP.

He's done worrying about his weight, cholesterol, and blood pressure. He's going to enjoy what little life he has left by doing just whatever the hell makes him feel good. His current pinched frugal life isn't worth spending the remaining years of his life living.

How do you know a man's given up?

The first thing to look for is how he dresses. Many men had to wear a suit or uniform all of their life's so when their done doing that they wear what makes them comfortable like old worn shirts hanging out over their beltline with convenient chest pockets for cell phones, cigars/cigarettes, notes, etc. They don't care how far their chest pockets droop down as long as they conveniently carry a whole bunch of crap they like to carry around.

They wear sans a belt pants or pants with generous waistlines with the comfortable fit of an elastic expanding beltline. He prefers not to press his pants or keep them very clean because they're for fit and function not to look competent or to attract the opposite sex. He's done with that.

His belt is leather with many worn holes for adjusting as his weight varies. His belt buckle is either plan or garish. There isn't anything in between. The plane belt buckle types want to keep a low profile and really don't give a shit what he thinks of himself whereas the garish belt buckle type wants to display to himself what he appreciates.

His shoes are comfortable and that's it. He doesn't need work boats because he doesn't endanger his feet any more. He doesn't wear dress shoes because he doesn't get dressed-up any more. He doesn't wear athletic shoes because he's well beyond being athletic. He wears shoes that are cheap and comfortable; there are no other considerations.

You can confirm who they are by looking into to their carts at the grocery store. Just look. You'll see bricks of butter, fatty steaks, bacon, hamburgers, white bread, greasy frozen french fries, cheap frozen dinners, candy, slabs of cheap cheese, Salisbury steaks, sausages, potato chips, frozen pizza, cheap garish cakes, full-leaded soda, beer, wine, and you'll see bottles of whiskey in their car in the back trunk as they load their groceries.

He's shopping alone. That's his only excuse for buying stuff the government preaches will kill him. He's not on the fruit and vegetable band wagon any more because he fell-off when his wife died. She was in charge of buying groceries. She was the one who made sure he ate only low-fat turkey products. She was the one who made sure he ate low-cholesterol low triglycerides fats. She made sure he ate his daily requirement of fruits and vegetables and she was the only one who cared how he lived. She's gone now and he doesn't care.

His sole is aching to see her again. He won't see her if he keeps living so he's going to enjoy himself dieing.

When Did Morales Become Prejudices

A few days ago I heard about Russia passing laws making it illegal to teach homosexuality to children which is consistent with the morals of billions of people over thousands of years from all over the world and is consistent with the tenets of every major religion. Historically, homosexuality has been described as immoral and an abomination with punishments ranging from censure to execution.

The gist of the story was that athletes, etc. should boycott the Olympics because Russians are "homophobic", "intolerant", "mean spirited", "prejudice", "outdated", etc. The liberal media fed-off each other giving priority to the story over other events having to do with floods in India where thousands were homeless and many others either dead or missing, the use of Saran gas in Syria, the latest doings of our dysfunctional government, etc. The editors of every major news organization and media outlet except Fox dedicated significant resources to the story deciding that an issue of an extremely small minority was more important than the death and suffering of the majority.

When did the morals of billions of people become prejudices? How did the definition of morals change from the beliefs of what is right by the overwhelming majority to the beliefs of what is right by an extreme minority? When did overtly sexual behavior by teenage singers become art? When did the dysfunctional lifes of people become something that should be "celebrated" with

In My Time

T.V. series, movies, novels, etc. When did people who hold traditional morals become "homophobes", "mean-spirited", "prejudice", "dangerous", "anti-democracy", "ignorant, etc.? When did people who morally disagree with an act become targets for sanctions that were once applied to people who committed the same act?

This is a significant change in public discourse because it's allowed dysfunctional people existing on the fringes of societies to have an inordinate amount of influence on the moral behavior of an entire society. This causes a tyranny of the minority where they compel the majority to support their morals to the detriment of the host society.

People who were traditionally sanctioned for immoral behavior are now in the position of sanctioning the majority for their moral behavior.

A society will not survive if it allows an extreme minority to continually disrupt its core morals. It will collapse devolving into self-centered adversarial groups or there'll be a backlash by the majority to reestablish traditional society to the extreme detriment to the minority.

Unfortunately, neither alternative is pleasant.

Dot, Dot, Dot (…) People

Dot, dot, dot(…)people are extremely annoying...Dot, dot, dot, people type … at the end of every statement in a text or email signifying that what they're trying to communicate is much more complicated and extensive than what can be typed…Dot, dot, dot people are very self-centered, shallow, not very intelligent, and obnoxious…Stop it...You piss me and others off…Can't you simply type a period than double space at the end of a cogent complete sentence…I mean do you really have to type … at the end of every statement…Can't you simply type a declarative sentence with a period at the end and leave it at that…Do you really think your simple little brain could think of something so complicated that you'd have to legitimately type … at the end of it…Don't you know that I consider people who type … at the end of every statement impolite, ignorant, disorganized, and unable to communicate what's in their very limited capacity brains…Don't you know that typing … at the end of your stupid sentences indicates to me that you think what you're typing is really smart when in actuality it's evidence of your ignorance and dumb-shittnish…So stop it already…It pisses me off…Oh and by the way is it too much to ask that you use even rudimentary punctuation or at a minimum break up you dumbass comments into paragraphs…You know what paragraphs are don't you…Well I've said enough already…Unfortunately, dot, dot, dot people are full of themselves and even if they read this wouldn't think it was referring to them but would laugh because they'd think the problem was that other people don't know how to use … properly…

In My Time

I Don't Have Pictures of Me Naked

There was a huge brew-ha-ha the other day over hottie young actresses who had their "Cloud"1 accounts hacked and pictures of themselves naked stolen and posted on the Internet.

Everyone I talked too, the media, government officials, analysts, pundits, etc. missed the point. All they talked about was how the Internet wasn't secure and how people should be vigilant about security.

Not one person that I heard asked:

Who has pictures of themselves naked? (…and if they do they should be ashamed of themselves. What would their mothers think?)

Why do they have pictures of themselves naked?

If someone has pictures of themselves naked why would they have them in a digital format and stored on their computer and in the "Cloud"?

Are pictures where one is naked a standard work in a young actresses oeuvre?

In My Time

Don't worry. I don't have pictures of me naked either in hardcopy or electronic formats.

What concerns me is that the morality of young women with pictures of themselves naked is not questioned nor considered abnormal. It's like if sex tapes were released and no one questioned the morality of the tapes existing. As if all they'd talk about was where the tape was produced and who released it. Oh wait. That's already been done. Anyways…

Everything old is new again. The "Cloud" is a very old concept. In the bad old days it was centralized computing. You had a central computer with dumb terminals connected. You have the same thing with the "Cloud" except dumb terminals have been replaced with smarter computers. The "Cloud" is an example of an old concept dusted-off and sold to an ignorant populace. Another example is re-releasing The Lord of the Rings every ten years with new cover art and new formats, i.e. movies. Youngsters think it was just created.

Shelter in Place

I was listening to the news the other day about a criminally dangerous bad guy running loose somewhere in the Northeast. Political and law enforcement authorities and the media advised the good citizens of the community to "Shelter in Place".

Yup, I'm not kidding. They advised law-abiding citizens to cower in their homes until more Manly Fellows apprehended the bad guy. I figuratively laughed my ass-off. Are you kidding me? Shelter in Place? Not on your life Brohiem.

I was thinking how funny it would be if someone tried to tell Texans that they should cower in their homes while a criminal was running loose. Texans train, plans, and preys for the day they can legally shoot someone with their thoughtfully selected and lovingly maintained weapons of choice. To be so delusional to think you could tell Texans to pass-up the opportunity to legally shoot someone is crazy clueless.

Texans are Manly Fellows who'd aggressively hunt down the criminal and shoot him dead. (I write him because

In My Time

Texans don't shoot women unless they really deserve it.) They'd be fully armed standing out in their yards preying for the opportunity to shoot the bad guy and if they did shoot him for the rest of their lives they'd be proudly telling the story of how they bagged him. Sorta like a story a hunter tells about the biggest buck he's ever shot. The kind of story his wife, children, and friends have heard a thousand times and sigh in boredom every time he tells it.

No, no, no… men don't shelter in place. Woman, children, and mitches (male bitches) shelter in place. Men hunt down and bag their prey while enjoying a pleasantly satisfying outing hoping and preying that they'll be granted the blessing of doing it again.

Nope. Men don't Shelter in Place.

Something Only A Man Can Do

I was waiting in line to get my coffee when I observed a 400+ lbs. man crushing a chair while talking on his mobile. This man was so fat he had no neck. He couldn't' look down at his belly because his chin was embedded in a shelf of fat that was his chest. O.K. ya' get me? This guy was fat.

Anyways, this really fat guy was lecturing someone on the other end of his mobile about proper diet, what foods were good for you and when, how the maintenance of homeostasis is improved with the correct diet, what foods should be avoided, and on and on in a very forceful and authoritative tone. I could tell he was passionate about his subject and wanted the other person on the line to change their ways and be healthy.

I thought how only a 400+ lbs. morbidly obese man could get away with lecturing someone about diet. I suspect if he were a woman the person on the other end of the line would hang-up laughing. I know I would.

In My Time

Women In Parking Lots

I don't know if it's a recent phenomenon (I think not because women have been driving more or less safely for a number of years) but I've noticed that when I'm making my way through a parking lot I have much less trouble when men are at the wheels then women.

Many times I'll back out of a space and pull forward to meet a car coming my way. If it's a man it seems that there's some kind of extra sensory communication between us because regardless of what side of the parking lot we're on we'll maneuver past each other without any hesitation. Even when both of our vehicles won't fit through an area we'll know how to maneuver so we rotate around each other and be on our ways.

However, whenever I meet a woman in a parking lot they insist on staying in their lane regardless of how many times either one of us has to back up and turn to make it over to our lane. I've had situations where I couldn't turn sharp enough to make it past a bumper of a woman's vehicle and she'd just sit there looking at me waiting impatiently for me to sort myself out. All she'd have to do is back up a couple of feet to let me swing on by yet they rarely do. Women have a natural inclination to stay between the lines regardless of how harmless going outside the lines would be. Many times I'd motion to a woman to drive past me on the right and she'd look at me confused. Some women would understand but sit tight refusing to move making my life even more frustrating.

I think woman insisting on staying between the lines is a manifestation of their historic and sacred responsibility to be the bearer of Civilization. A good example of this is how the West was settled. The first to settle in an area were gold miners and/or ranchers. Along with or shortly after their arrival would come saloons and brothels to cater to the almost all male population. The few females were practicing the oldest profession. After a while they'd start calling it a town and more stores and such would open in a concentrated area forming a main street. About the time a main street was forming Ladies accompanied by their husbands or fathers, who were store keepers, preachers, doctors, lawyers, etc., would start moving in and taking interest in their communities. This interest manifested itself in building schools, churches, libraries, hospitals, etc. that were the backbones of civilized communities. In some cases the really fun places that men used to go too were closed down or made to tone down their activities causing the really fun people to pack-up and move farther West where they would plant the rotten seeds of a new community. They'd party hard until civilization caught up to them again then they'd move on eventually ending up in California where their spawn live as debauched as they did.

So I'm thinking the reason why women refuse to be creative in parking lots is because they have the sacred obligation to maintain a civilized society. If everyone just drove around parking lots willy-nilly anarchy and brothels would soon follow. I think that's also the reason why women in the fast food industry always delve out the exact proportions as delineated by company policy whereas men just slop it on and move on but that's a subject for another time.

Are You a Misandrist

From 2000 to the present the most common is the third response. Every time I make a positive statement about men someone feels compelled to voice an opposing negative statement. They just can't hold it in. The technical term for these people is "Man Beater".

When a Man Beater hears a positive statement about men they experience mental anguish because their psyche becomes unbalanced. The only way they can regain balance is by making counter negative statements. Unfortunately, most Man Beaters are lost causes because they've been irreversibly trained by misandrist groups to resist positive thoughts about men and are irrevocably committed to the maintenance and proliferation of the misandrist meme. Man Beaters are so well trained and so deeply immersed in the misandrist meme that it's nearly impossible to break them free. Man Beaters are lost soles destined to live in the Herd for their entire unexamined and thus worthless lives.

The misandrist meme is so pervasive that it lives-on rarely if ever being challenged. I watched a program on CNN where three ladies and a male moderator agreed unanimously that women are much better Intelligence Analyst than men because women are more patient and detail oriented whereas men are impatient, don't care about details, and are too action-oriented. There was no dissenting opinion.

I thought how significant is it that CNN aired this program without a dissenting opinion in favor of male Intelligence Analyst? Would CNN have aired a program with three men talking about how better Intelligence Analyst they are than women because they have a sense of urgency, stays out of the weeds and sees the "big-picture", and are results oriented? The show would never happen because it goes against the misandrist meme.

Here's another test especially for Christians. Read out loud the statement below.

Men are the leaders of their families.

Diagnostic Key:

1. Yes they are.
2. Yes, but they're not supposed to be abusive or dictatorial; should listen to their wives who are they're equals; should follow as often as they lead; should have an open mind; be even-tempered; and numerous other qualifying\discounting statements. Will also site bible passages out of context to support their biblically erroneous beliefs and site the dangers of wife and child abuse.
3. No they're not.

The misandrist meme has an active and robust life within the Christian community. Whenever the topic of men being leaders comes up there's usually a Man Beater or two about who are compelled to express responses 2 and 3. It never fails. It states clearly in the bible that men are leaders of their families yet many very good people who are Christians are Man Beaters completely unaware that they live in the Herd.

There's a significant dissonance between how men are and the dominant misandrist meme. The result of this dissonance is a society under stress because members of the society have to contend with the conflict between what they know to be true and the pervasive misandrist meme. One can only hope that the energy from this stress will be the force behind the birth of a new more Truthful meme.

In My Time

Dads' Vs. Moms' Humor

I drove into a Wal-Mart parking lot the other day and saw a father pushing a cart with his cute little curly headed boy sitting in the kids seat in the cart.

The little boy was looking around as the Favored Son.

His dad pushed the cart into a cart coral and said "See ya'" to the little boy and walked away leaving the little boy in the cart.

The boy watched as his father walked away. The boy looked around, then looked at his father becoming very confused. I could see the little boy was thinking wait a minute. What's going on here? Aren't I coming with you?

The father laughed and went back and got his son.

I got out of my car and said to the father, "You better not let his mother see that."

He said, "Oh no."

In My Time

I don't know of any mother who would see the humor in pretending to abandon their child.

It was really funny.

A Fall Day

The soft feeling of leafs returning to the cold dead ground.

Crisp clean air smelling of vegetation decaying into the Earth.

The Sky dark and brooding waiting its time to Rein.

Ominous grey clouds overhead warning of cold snowy months ahead.

Leafs hanging dead in their colorful glory waiting for Mother Nature to complete their Cycle of Life. Longing to return to Earth where they came.

A deeply pleasant anticipation of months of cold and snowy weather ahead challenging your Spirit.

Looking forward to precious time spent with family and friends bundled in warm homes with frosty windows on the outside and dewy windows on the inside evidence of sumptuous meals being prepared. Dinners prepared by the Woman in your life who feels a satisfying need to serve you while you watch hours and hours of FOOTBALL. A time when you and your Woman enjoy spending time together yet comfortably apart.

Fall reminds me of Football games played in the high school stadium near my childhood home in Northeast New York. I remember hearing the sounds of bands playing and the gentle roar of the crowd flowing into the chilly clear night to me in my backyard. I didn't know that in the years ahead I'd play on the same field creating sounds for the next generation to hear.

Fall is a Man's Season. It's when football, hunting, and Mother Nature combine challenging Men to live. It's when our necks swell, our muscles seem to be harder, and we fell GOOD! Damned GOOD! It's when the Woman in our life look especially fetching.

Fall is when the chaos of the year ends and a more introspective and restful time begins.

Falls the time of year to slow-down and be proud of your accomplishments and plan for new challenges in the year ahead. A time when you fix your life in time and come to understand how you're living it.

Fall is when the furious activities of survival take a time out. It's when what's happened has happened and you are consoled to the outcome.

It took many years to know why I loved the Fall. After years of thought I learned Fall represents death. Death is required for life to renew in the Spring. Without Death, there is no new life.

Men are animals. Our brain knows we are; it's our minds and society that denies it.

In My Time

If we would listen to our brains we'd slow-down, feast, drink, make babies, and look forward to restful months of quiet thought. The year's harvest is in; we should enjoy the rewards.

Most Men continue to do what they do all year filling Fall with mindless activities taking short impotent pauses on holidays to reminisce but not to Think.

This Fall make a promise to yourself that you'll stop and spend time to understand who you are as a Man and who you want to become.

Do it for yourself and, more importantly, do it for your Family.

In My Time

My Car Leaks Oil

I was at a Quicki Lube type place having my car's oil changed.

A pretty little Blondee teenager screeched-up and bopped out of her car up to the Attendant.

The Attendant asked her what kind of oil change she wanted.

Blondee asked what kinds are there.

The Attendants said, (I paraphrase) there's Regular, Gold, and Platinum level services.

Blondee says after thinking very seriously, "I think my cars leaking oil so it better be the Platinum level."